AF574711

MYSTERIOUS ENGLAND

JOHN CURTIS

Text by Richard Ashby

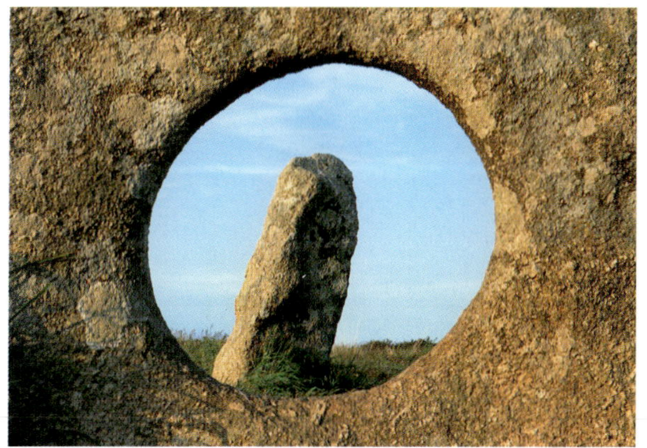

SALMON

INTRODUCTION

The early missionaries who attempted to convert England to Christianity no doubt intended to drive out the old religions completely. Old shrines were abandoned and pulled down and many ancient rituals suppressed. But the task was too difficult; the old beliefs were ingrained and the physical remains often too extensive to destroy. No doubt the population also resisted these unwelcome changes. One result was that ancient sites were often Christianised; for instance, a church would be built within a prehistoric circle or a pagan well would become associated with a Christian Saint. But in other, perhaps more remote, places, the old religion would survive. Even today the visitor will be startled by the presence of votive offerings at a remote well or at the base of a standing stone.

The original purpose of many of these sites is quite often unknown and many have become associated with local lore and legend. How much of this is authentic cannot now be told, but stories about the devil and his activities abound, as do legends of King Arthur, embellished by Malory and Tennyson, and no doubt many places were keen to be associated with this great mythical figure, Britain's 'once and future king'. These ancient sites and their continuing veneration today show the power of the spiritual, which breaks through sometimes, even in our post-Christian and largely secular society. But however rational we may think we are, at many of the sites of mysterious England it is possible to experience something of the awe that our ancestors must have felt in the presence of the great unknown.

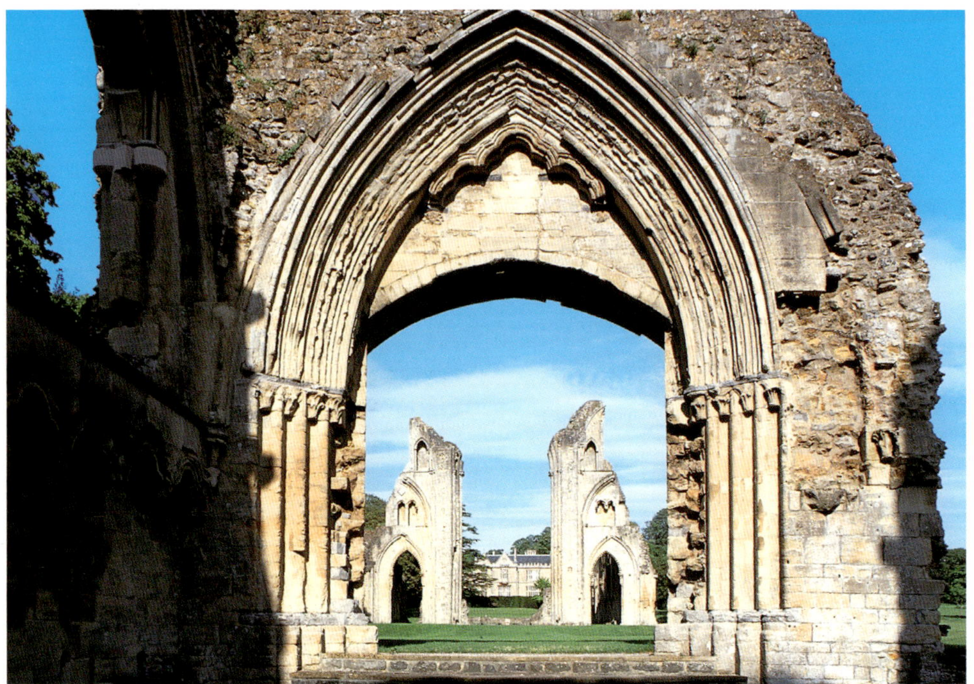

GLASTONBURY ABBEY, *Somerset*

Glastonbury has been a sacred spot for almost two thousand years. Legend has it that Jesus was brought here as a young man by Joseph of Arimathea, as famously alluded to in William Blake's poem 'Jerusalem', and that Joseph returned here as the first Christian missionary to Britain. The Glastonbury Thorn which flowers, unusually, at Christmas-time, is said to have sprouted when Joseph struck his staff into the ground. The nearby Tor is identified as the Isle of Avalon, where King Arthur was taken to recover from the fatal wound received in his last battle. In 1191 the monks of the abbey claimed that they had discovered the bodies of Arthur and his Queen and re-buried them in their church, which became a great centre of pilgrimage.

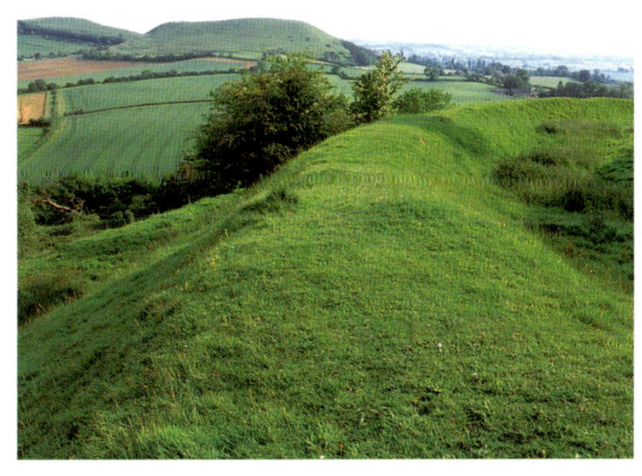

CADBURY CASTLE, *South Cadbury, Somerset*

It is a fairly recent tradition that this hill fort, fortified and re-fortified over many centuries, was the Camelot of Arthurian legend. It was given authority only in the 16th century when the historian John Leland first suggested that this was the location of Camelot, though he may have been drawing on an earlier tradition. Glastonbury Tor is clearly visible across the Somerset Levels.

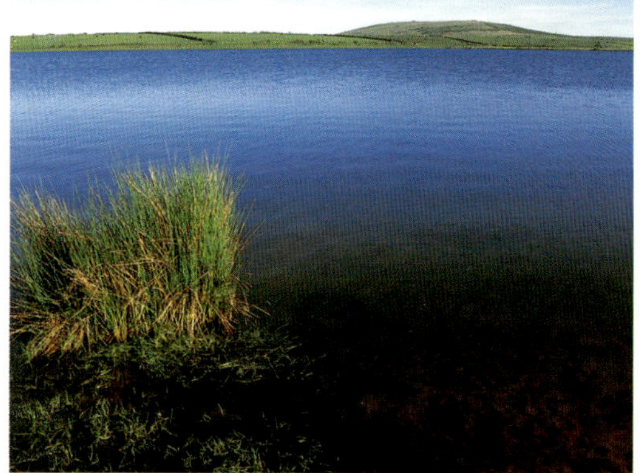

DOZMARY POOL, *Bolventor, Cornwall*
Merlin brought the young King Arthur to this place high on Bodmin Moor where the 'Lady of the Lake' presented him with the sword Excalibur. It had to be returned here but Sir Bedivere, acting for the dying King, twice failed in his task. At the third attempt, a white hand emerged as he threw the sword, caught it and disappeared beneath the waters.

TINTAGEL, *Cornwall*
Away from the village is the castle of Tintagel, famed as the supposed birthplace of King Arthur and with its associations with Uther Pendragon, (Arthur's father), Merlin and Tristan and Isolde. It was the 12th century historian, Geoffrey of Monmouth, who first placed Arthur here in his *'History of the Kings of England'*. His ideas were taken up and incorporated into the accounts by Malory and later by Tennyson. There is evidence of occupation from the 5th century but the castle itself dates from Norman times. It has been badly damaged over the centuries by the sea and is today a picturesque ruin, but with its high cliffs, roaring seas and 'Merlin's Cave' at its base it is an impressive and magnificent place.

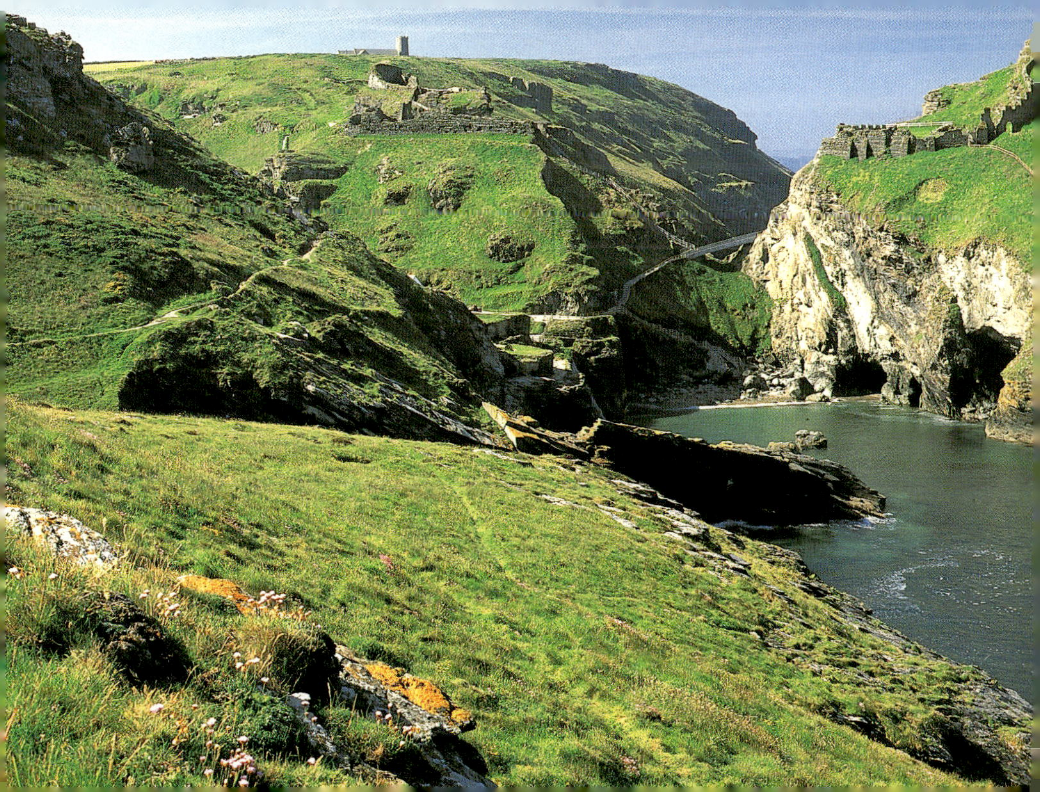

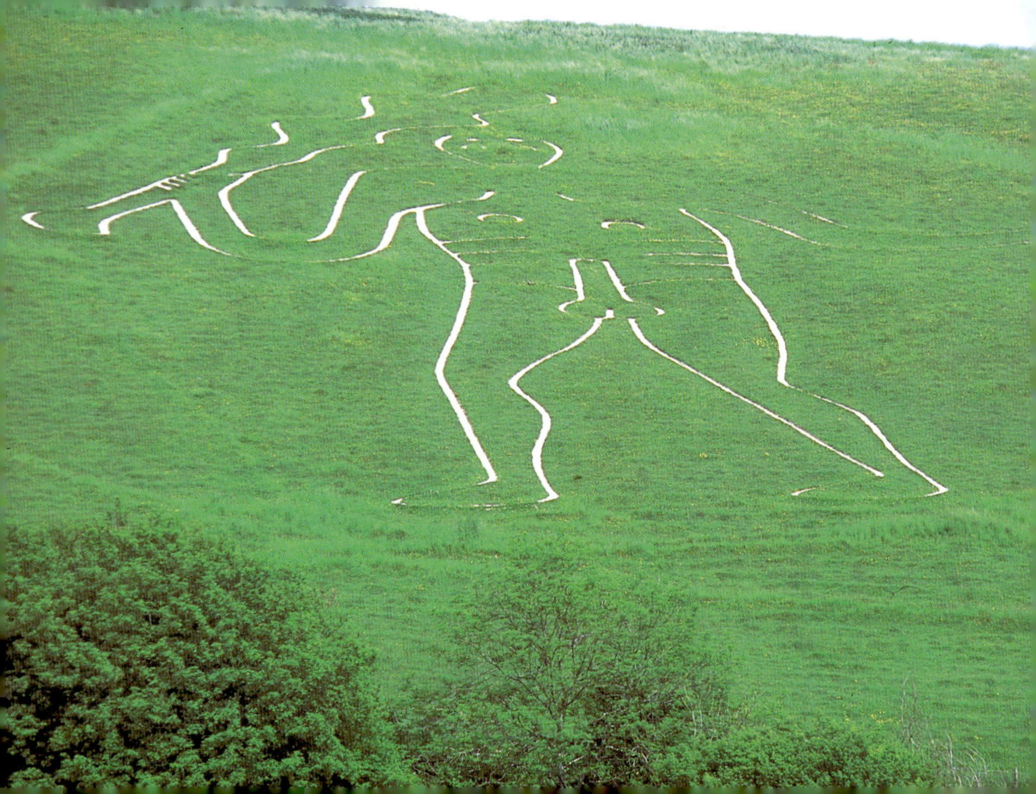

CERNE GIANT, *Cerne Abbas, Dorset*
The earliest written record of this extraordinarily virile figure dates only to 1751. Experts, however, say that the figure is much older than that and may well be of Roman times or even older. It may represent Hercules, since there is some evidence that he originally carried an animal skin in his left hand and might well have been cut in connection with a revival of the cult of the hero. Naturally, with such a figure, there is an associated fertility cult and barren women were said to conceive after sleeping here. The Victorians erased the erect phallus by filling in its outline with earth and grass but it has subsequently been restored to its original proud state.

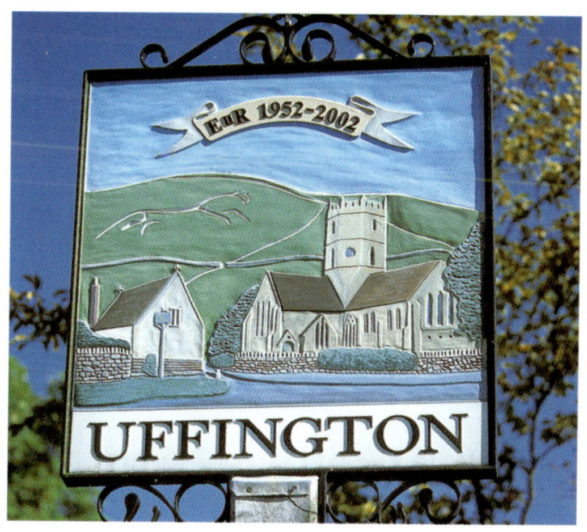

WHITE HORSE, UFFINGTON, *Oxfordshire*
The elegant stylised White Horse shown here on the village sign, dates back to the late Bronze Age, and may be connected to local tribal worship of a horse goddess. Some say that it is a dragon and commemorates the triumph of St George on a hill nearby.

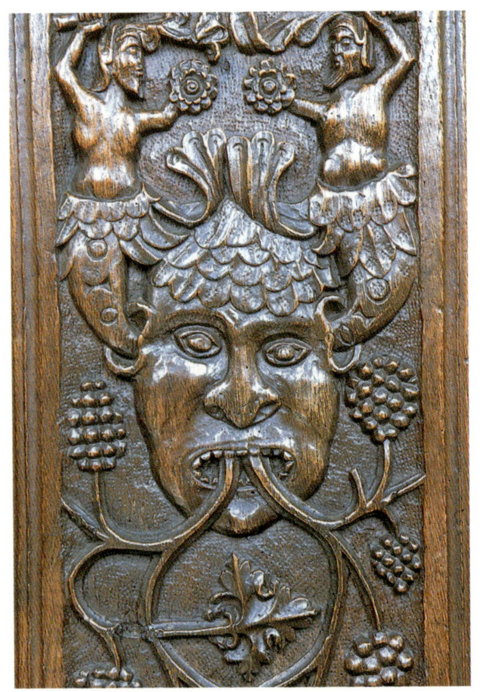

CROWCOMBE CHURCH, *Somerset*

This image of a head from which sprouts leaves, but with no body, is found in many churches and cathedrals across England, usually carved on a 'boss' in the roof or on the capital of a pillar. It may well have been a pre-Christian Celtic god of fertility, but why he is so common in churches is something of a mystery.

UPPER SHERINGHAM CHURCH, *Norfolk*

The very fine figures of people and animals carved on the 15th century bench-ends here include a cat and a baby in swaddling clothes and this one of a mermaid, a most unusual representation in a church. One story says that it commemorates a mermaid who was denied entry to a service because of the general belief that mermaids had no soul.

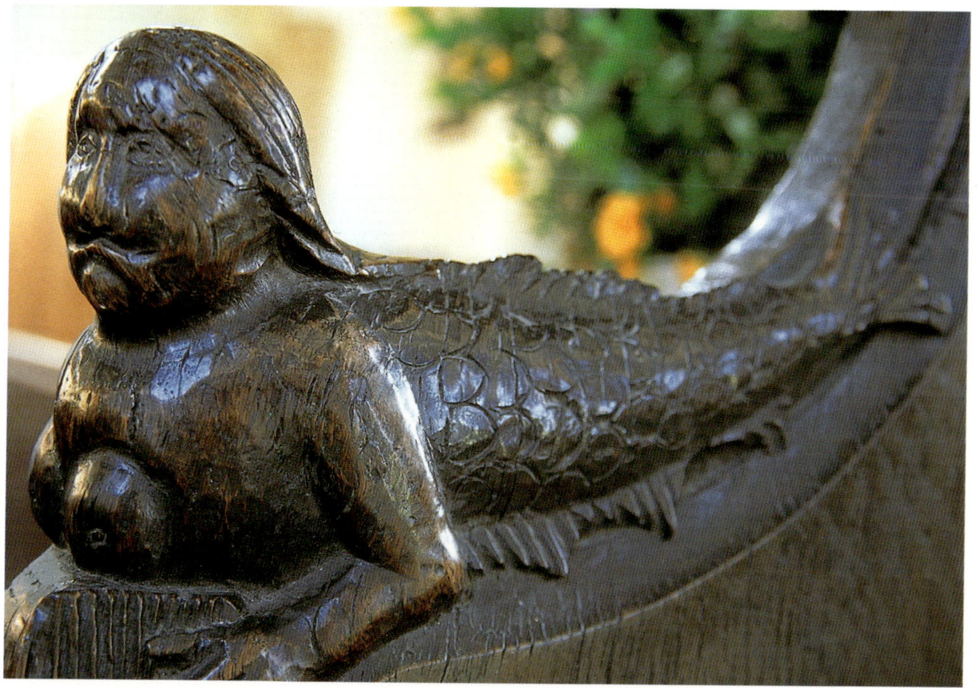

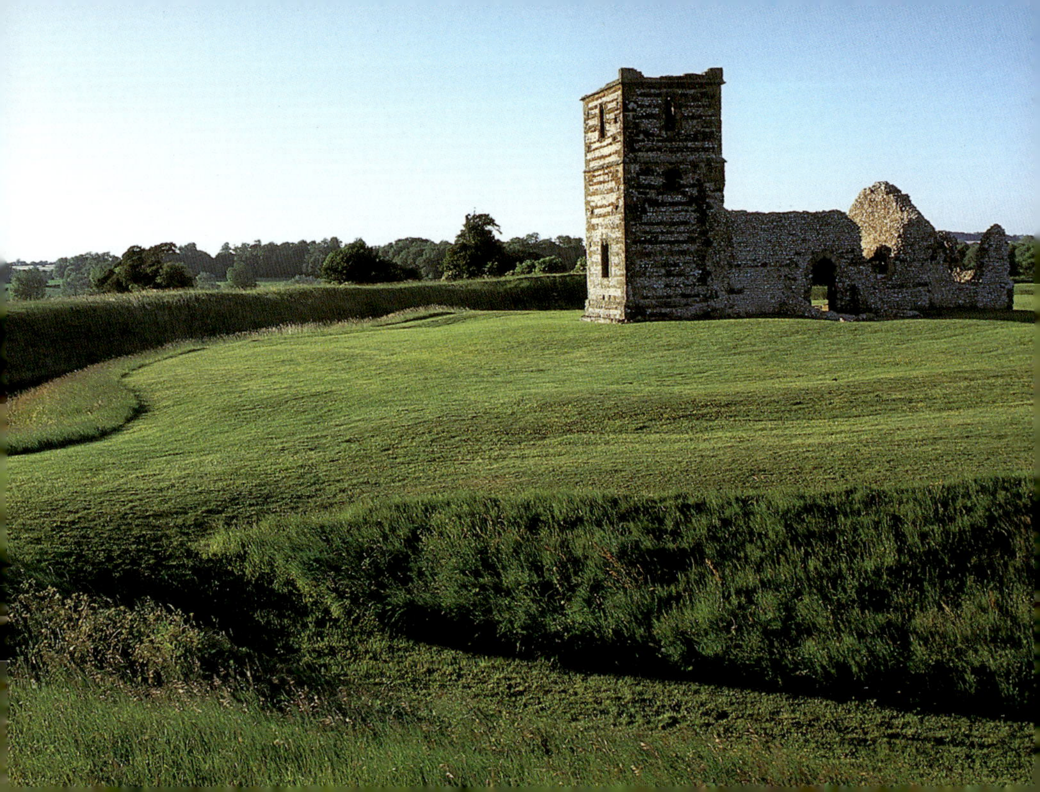

KNOWLTON RINGS, *Dorset*

As Christianity swept across England it was quite common for pagan sites to be adapted or converted to the use of the new religion. At Knowlton a 12th century church is built within the largest of four Bronze Age earth circles in an area where there are many other burial mounds and ditches. The church remained in use until around 1747 when it was abandoned.

RUDSTONE MONOLITH, *East Yorkshire*

Nearly 26ft high, this is the tallest standing stone in England and was once the centre of ritual worship of the ancient inhabitants of this area. The name derives from the old English word 'Rood', meaning 'cross', and this monolith, now capped with lead, was probably once topped by a wooden cross by the early missionaries who tried to Christianise this ancient site.

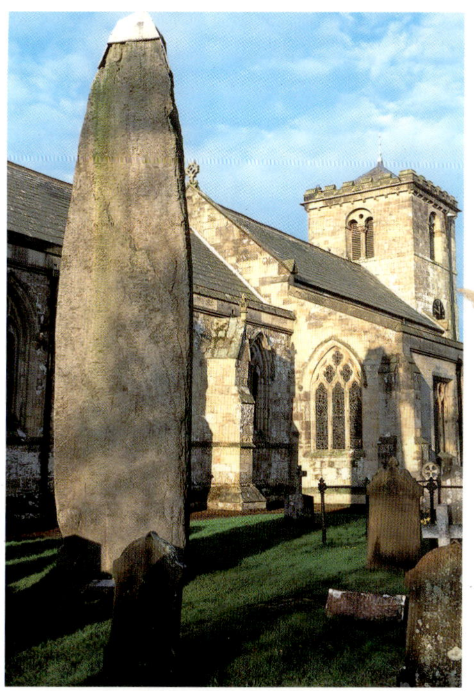

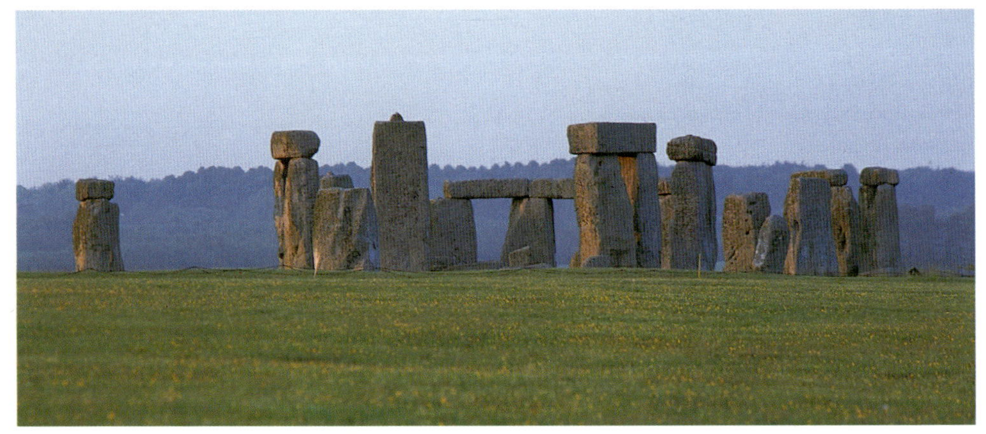

STONEHENGE, *Wiltshire*
Attracting many thousands of visitors each year, Stonehenge is the centre of 'Druidical' rites and the place of pilgrimage for 'Hippy' and 'New Age' travellers at the summer solstice. Its scale is still overwhelming today, yet no one really knows how or why Stonehenge was built.

AVEBURY STONE CIRCLE, *Wiltshire*
Avebury, with its great circular bank and ditch and stones standing in great circles and avenues, is one of the largest prehistoric monuments in Europe. It is said that the stones represented the head and body of a serpent passing through a circle, although its purpose is lost in the mists of time.

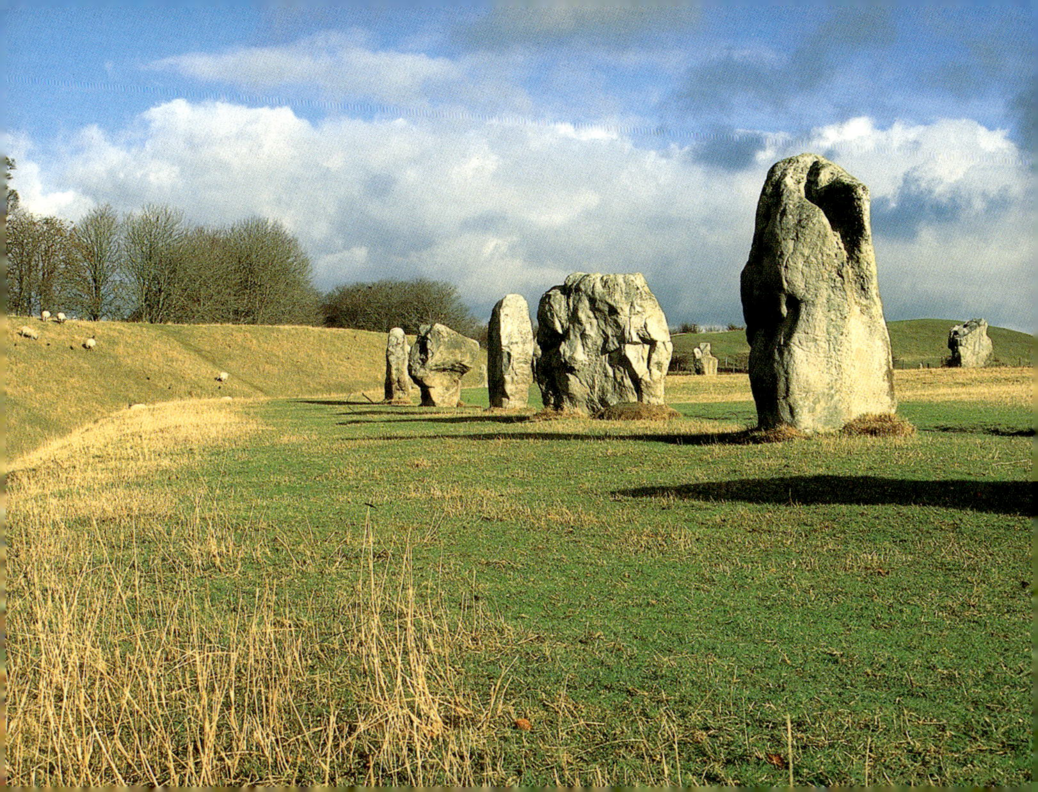

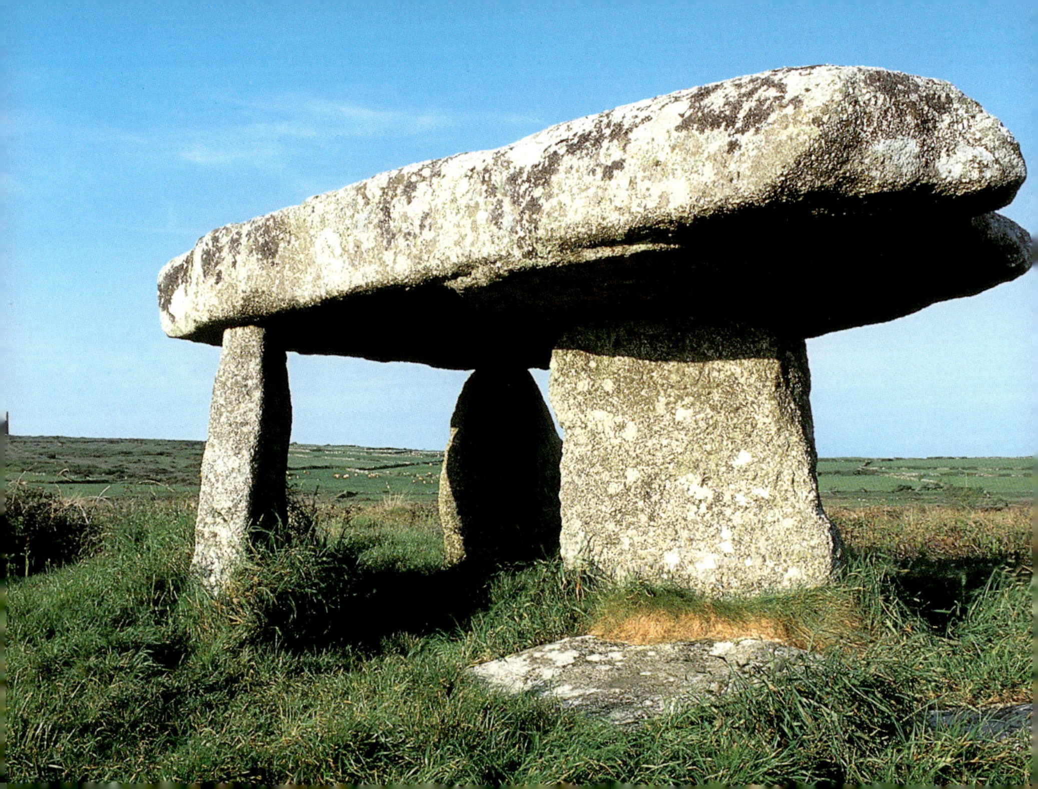

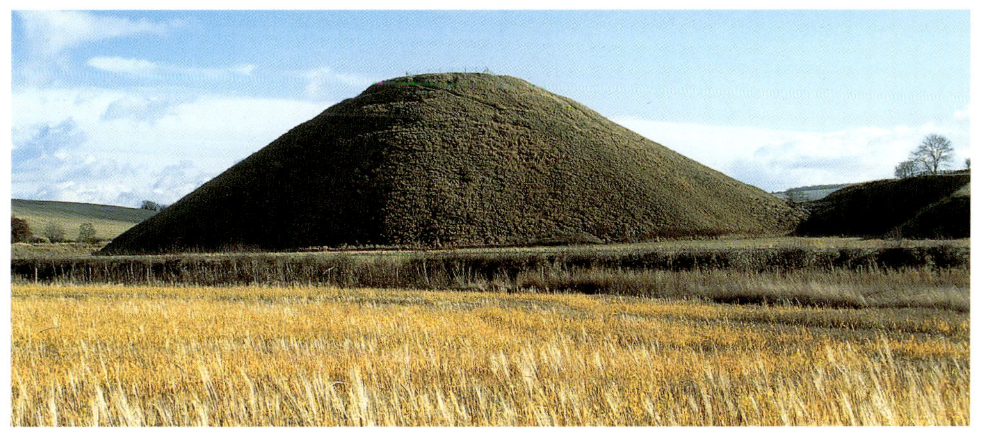

LANYON QUOIT, *Madron, Cornwall*
'Quoits' are believed to be the great stones of a Neolithic burial chamber now exposed after the surrounding earth has been eroded over the centuries. The heavy capstone here was originally supported on four uprights and was reputedly high enough for a man on horseback to ride underneath.

SILBURY HILL, *Wiltshire*
Dating from around 2660BC, Silbury Hill may have some association with Avebury nearby. It might be the burial chamber of King Sil or perhaps it was a solar observatory. No one knows. There have been three attempts to excavate the hill but nothing has ever been found.

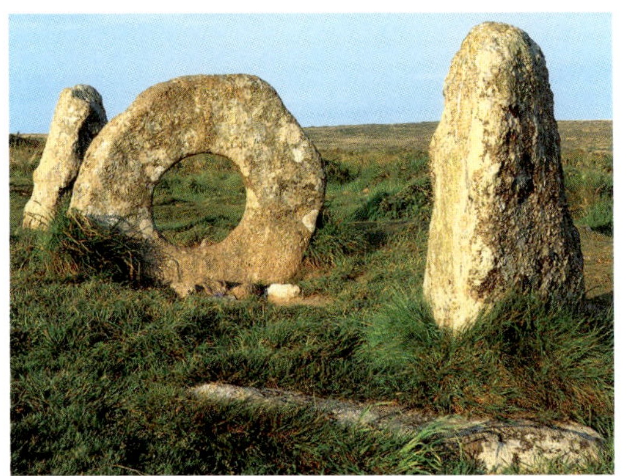

MEN-AN-TOL, *Morvah, Cornwall*

Originally believed to be a tomb, recent thinking suggests that these stones were part of a circle having ritual or astronomical purposes. Local superstition has it that the central stone has healing powers and that by passing a naked child through the hole three times it would be cured of rickets and scrofula. Like many such structures, Men-an-Tol retains its mystery.

MITCHELL'S FOLD,
Stapeley Hill, Shropshire

Close to the Welsh border and with fine views into Shropshire and Wales is this Bronze Age circle dating from around 2000BC. There were originally some 30 stones, of which 15 still stand. The story is that a magic cow lived here which would give milk to any passer-by. The cow was greatly angered by a wicked witch who milked it into a bucket full of holes and thus wasted the milk. The cow realised what was happening, kicked the bucket away and turned the witch into stone. Local people encircled her with more standing stones so she could not escape. The antiquarian William Stukeley thought that it was here that the young Arthur drew the sword from the stone, thus showing that he was the rightful King of Britain.

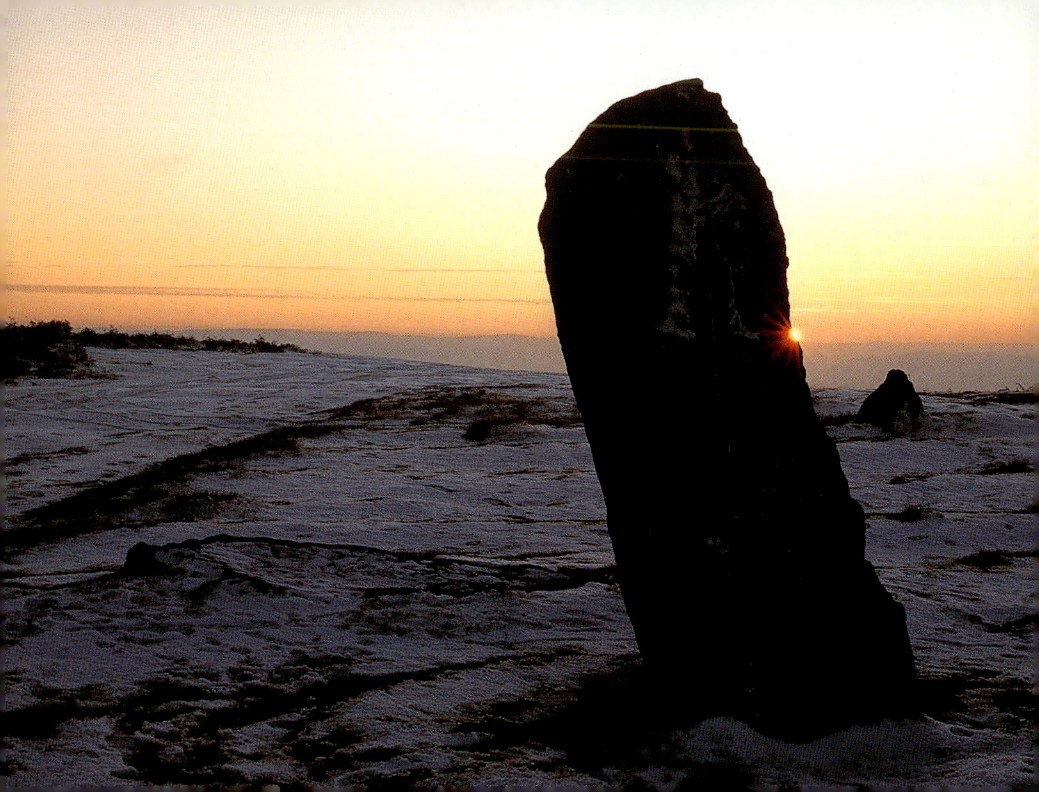

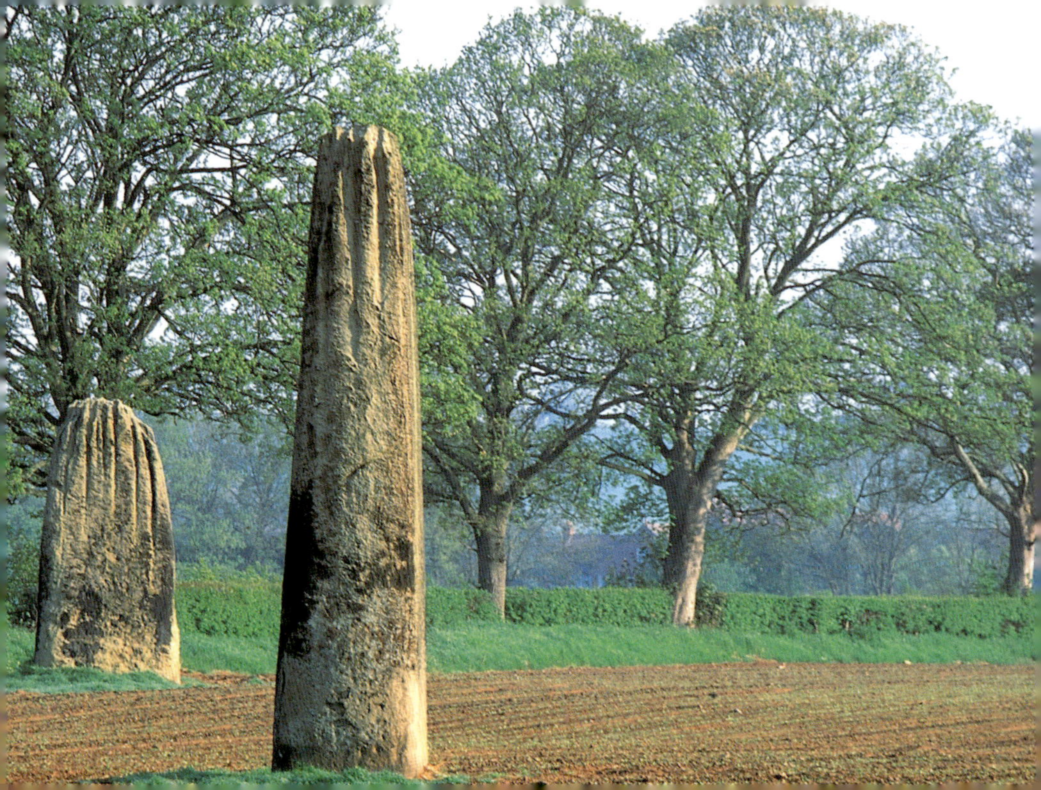

DEVIL'S ARROWS,
Boroughbridge, North Yorkshire
In popular lore the arrival of Christianity to the shores of England brought about a life or death struggle with the Devil himself. In a number of places the stories of the wrath of the Devil explained what we now know to have other origins. Here it is said that the Devil, standing on Howe Hill (near where Fountains Abbey is now) threw these stones at the Christian settlement of Aldborough, but missed, and they fell here. There were once more stones: the antiquarian John Leland recorded seeing four in the 1530s but thirty years later another traveller, William Campden, said that one of the stones had been destroyed in the search for treasure. Three stones survive.

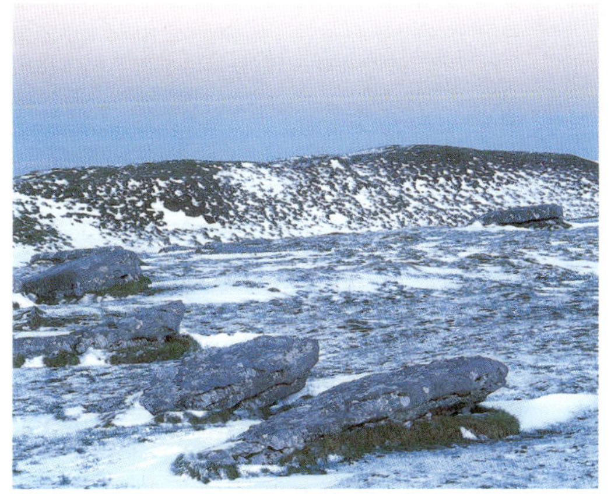

ARBOR LOW, *near Bakewell, Derbyshire*
Constructed around 2500BC, this stone circle is sometimes referred to as 'The Stonehenge of the Peak District'. 46 large stones and 13 smaller ones lie flat within a circular bank or 'henge', looking from above like a massive clock face. There is no evidence as to why it was constructed or for what it was used.

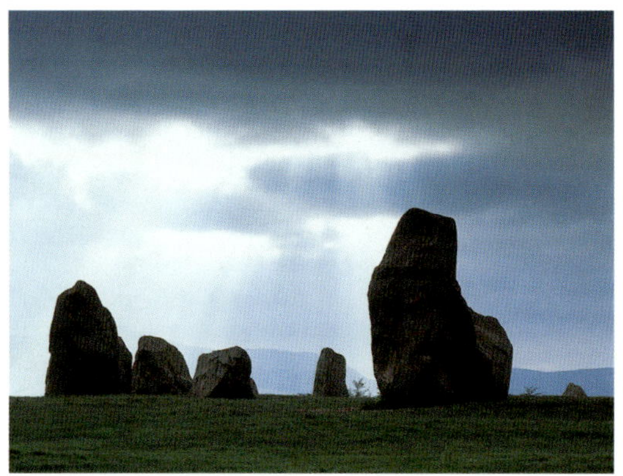

CASTLERIGG STONE CIRCLE,

Keswick, Cumbria

Castlerigg occupies a striking site set on the top of a low hill with views across to Skiddaw and Blencathra. 38 stones form the circle, while within it a further 10 make a square. Built around 3,000BC it is at its most impressive at sunset when the mystery and isolation of this site and the changing weather emphasise its spiritual power.

DOD LAW ROCK CARVINGS,

Doddington, Northumberland

What are these marks incised on the flat surface of exposed rocks in this hill-top moor with its views towards the Cheviot Hills? Many are in the shape of a cup surrounded by rectangles and there are circles and other grooves in the stone. Is this 'art' done by an ancient tribe for their pleasure or is there another deeper meaning connected to ritual or worship which has been lost over the centuries? There are many explanations but no one knows. However the whole area was clearly an important place for the local inhabitants since there is an Iron Age hill fort nearby and there were once many stone circles and barrows here. Cup and ring carvings exist in other parts of the country, but these at Dod Law are particularly well preserved and easily accessible.

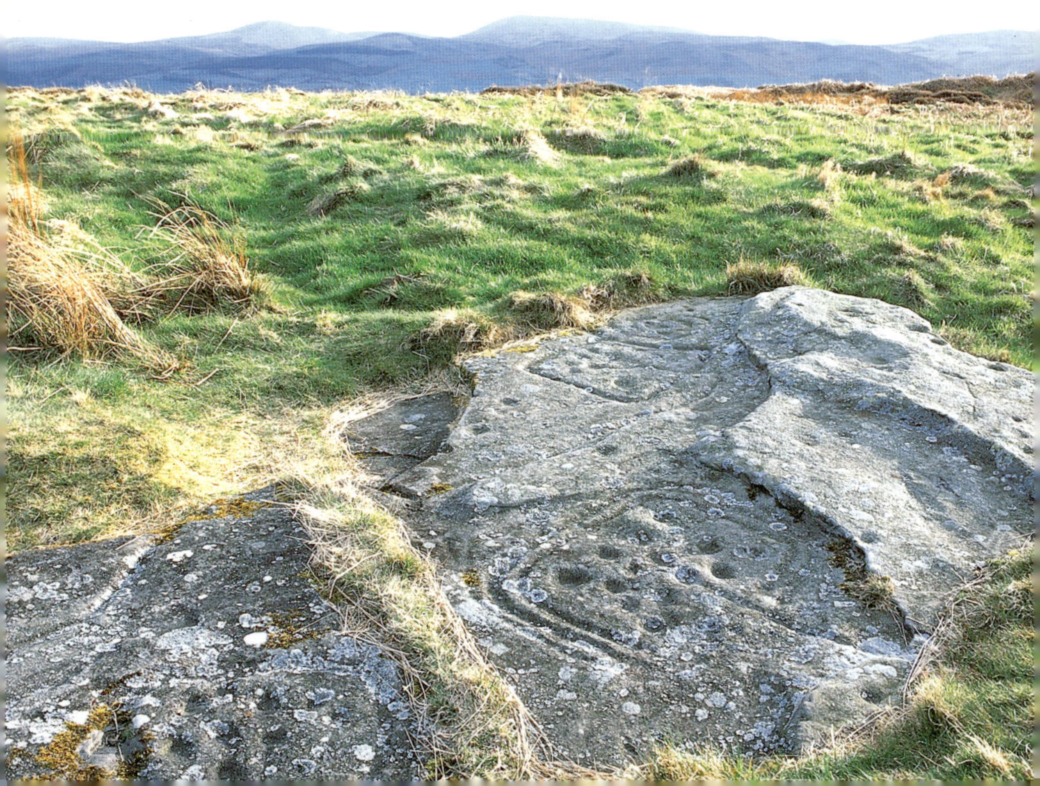

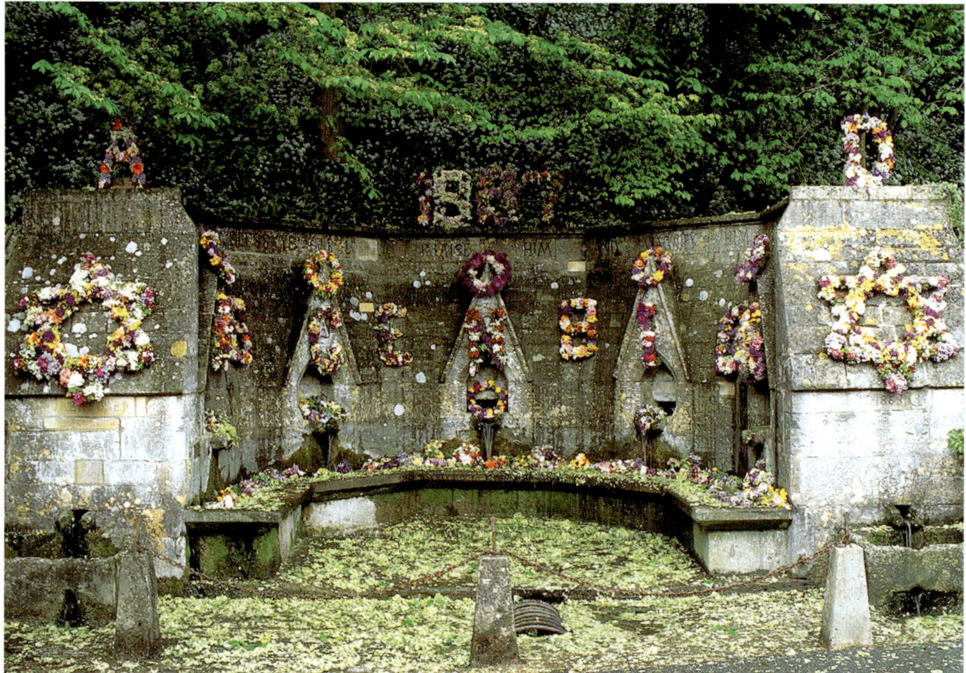
PRAISE HIM AND

DRESSED WELLS, *Bisley, Gloucestershire*
Fresh, clean water is an essential to healthy living and it is no wonder that villagers have given thanks for its provision. In Derbyshire well-dressing is an old tradition, but at Bisley it dates back only to 1863 when the local Vicar took it upon himself to transform the village water supply into the 'Seven Wells' and to begin the service of thanksgiving, which continues today.

DRESSED TREE, *Aston-on-Clun, Shropshire*
On the last weekend of May the people of this pretty Shropshire village celebrate 'Arbor Day' when the Black Poplar in the centre of the village is decorated and is the focus for great festivities. Tree dressing may well date back to pagan times but perhaps may also be associated with the Restoration of Charles II who decreed that May 29th should be named – 'Oak Apple Day'.

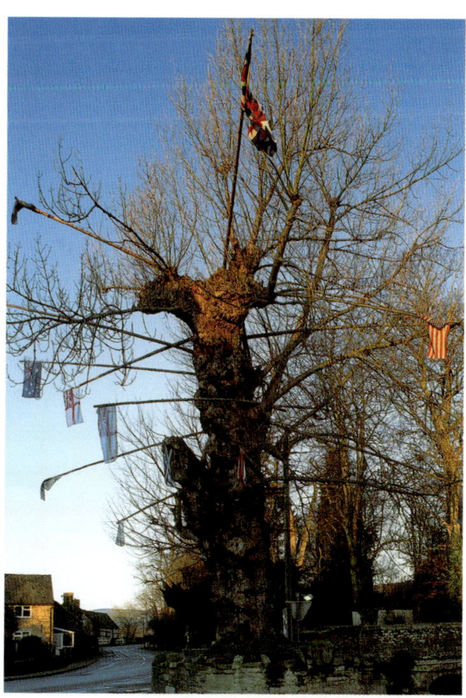

ST CLETHER'S WELL, *Cornwall*

There are over 200 holy wells in Cornwall. Probably all have pre-Christian significance and many were subsequently incorporated into Christian worship. This must be one of the most beautiful. There was a chapel here on Bodmin Moor in the 5th century, though the present building dates from the 15th. It is situated on a hillside, along a path and some distance from the parish church and the nearest road. The spring bubbles up from its own little structure nearby. The water flows into the chapel, passing under the granite altar and past the alcove which possibly once held the bones of the Saint, and out across the sloping field to the River Inney below. It is a place of great peace.

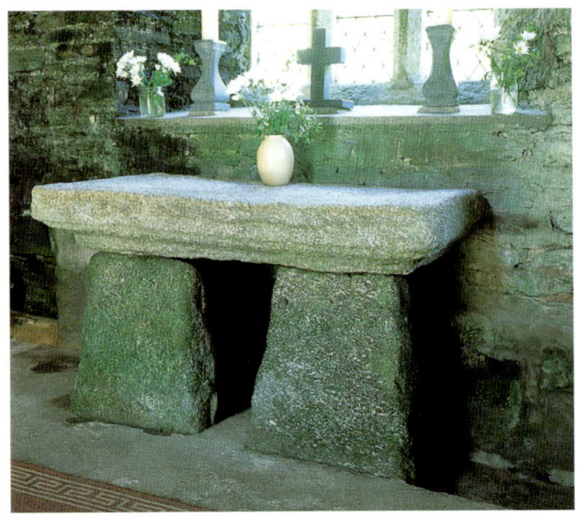

MADRON WELL, *Cornwall*

It is an ancient tradition to tear off a piece of cloth (or 'Cloutie') from the afflicted part of a sick person's body and to hang it on a tree. As it rots, so the hurt will disappear. The custom still survives, and here the boughs of the tree above the holy well are covered with such tokens.

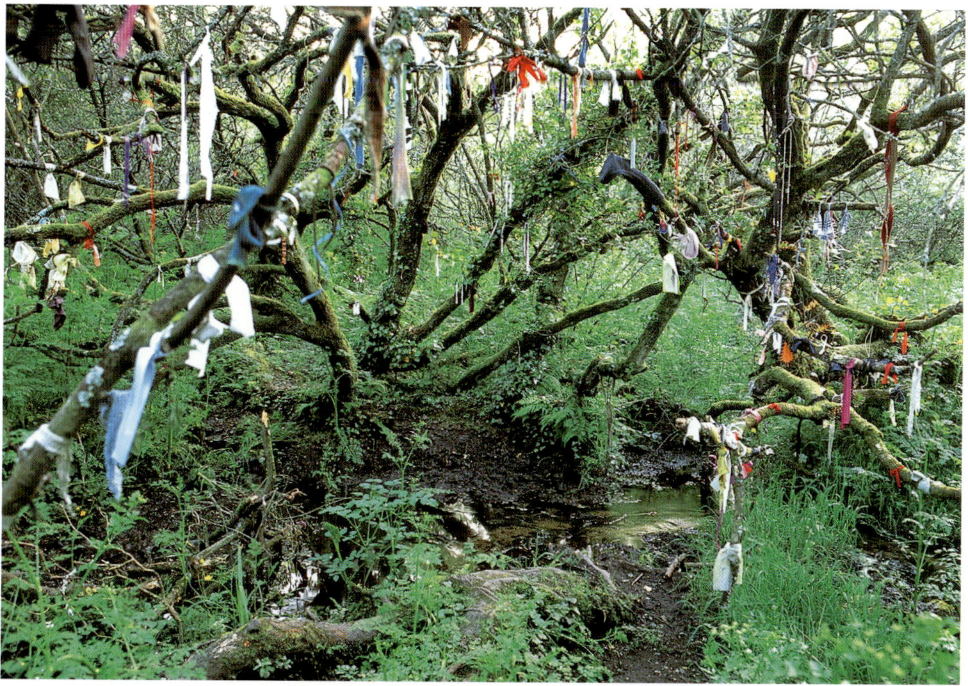

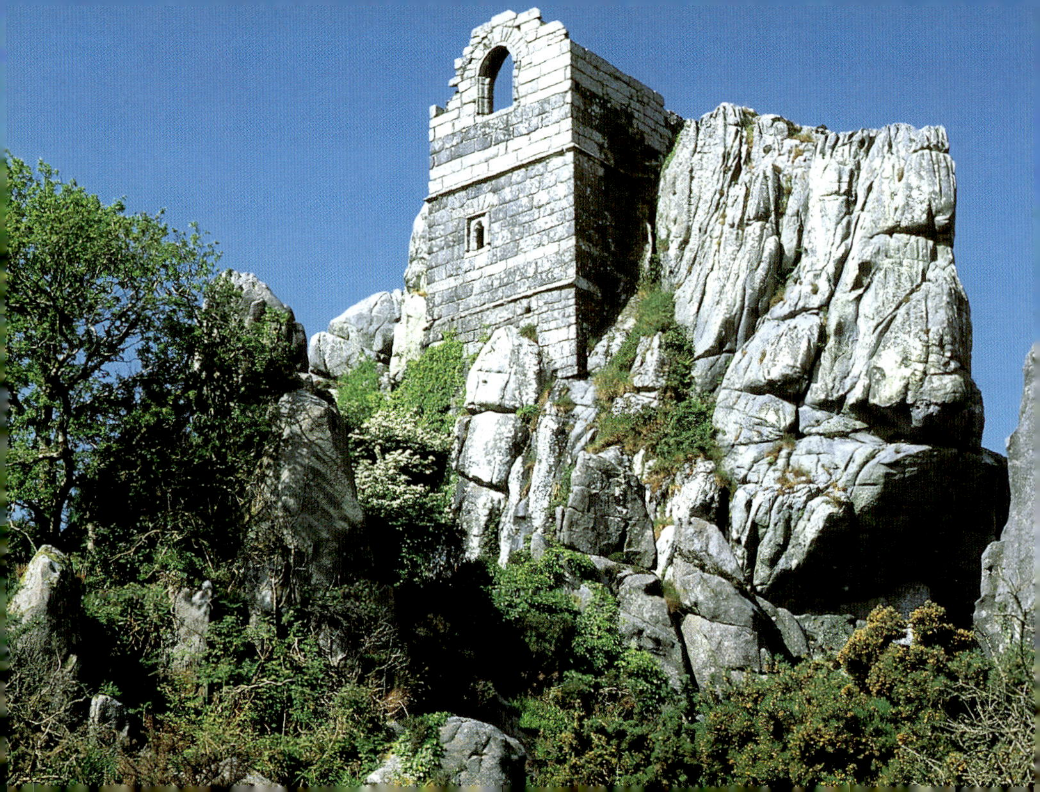

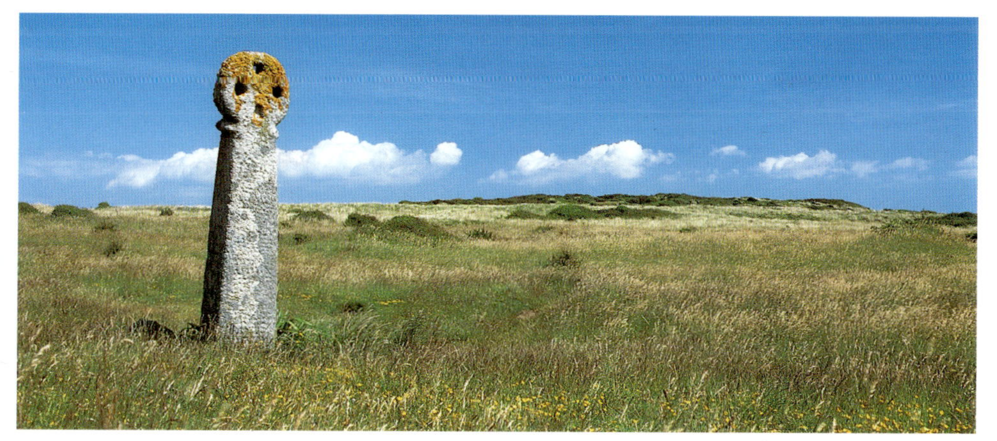

ST MICHAEL'S CHAPEL, *Roche, Cornwall*
Built in a spectacular setting on a rocky outcrop, St Michael's Chapel was a place of refuge for lepers, and the Cornish Saint, Gundred, tended her father here. The doomed lovers, Tristan and Isolde, found refuge in the hermit's chapel, which is said to be haunted by a local tin miner.

ST PIRAN'S CROSS,
Penhale Sands, near Perranporth, Cornwall
St Piran, patron saint of Cornwall, is said to have sailed across the Irish sea on a millstone! This Celtic cross, unusual because it has only three holes, marks the spot where the Saint landed on Penhale Sands to begin his conversion of Cornwall to Christianity.

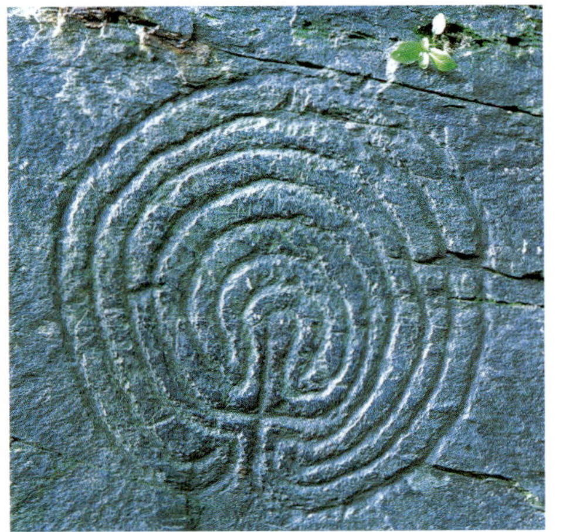

ROCK VALLEY MAZE,
near Tintagel, Cornwall

The history of these carvings is shrouded in mystery. Only discovered in 1948, it is not at all certain how old they are, but they may originate in the Bronze Age, or be the more recent work of local cloth workers!

JULIAN BOWER, *Alkborough, Lincolnshire*

This is a turf 'maze', or more correctly, a labyrinth, since there is only one path in and out and no dead ends. It was laid out in the 13th century by monks from a nearby Benedictine monastery. It is not known what these medieval labyrinths were used for, but they became quite common after the fall of Jerusalem made pilgrimage there impossible. It may well be that they represent some sort of 'The Way of the Cross' and were used for devotional and penitential purposes. After the Reformation it survived and was subsequently used by the local people as a site for village games on the eve of May Day.

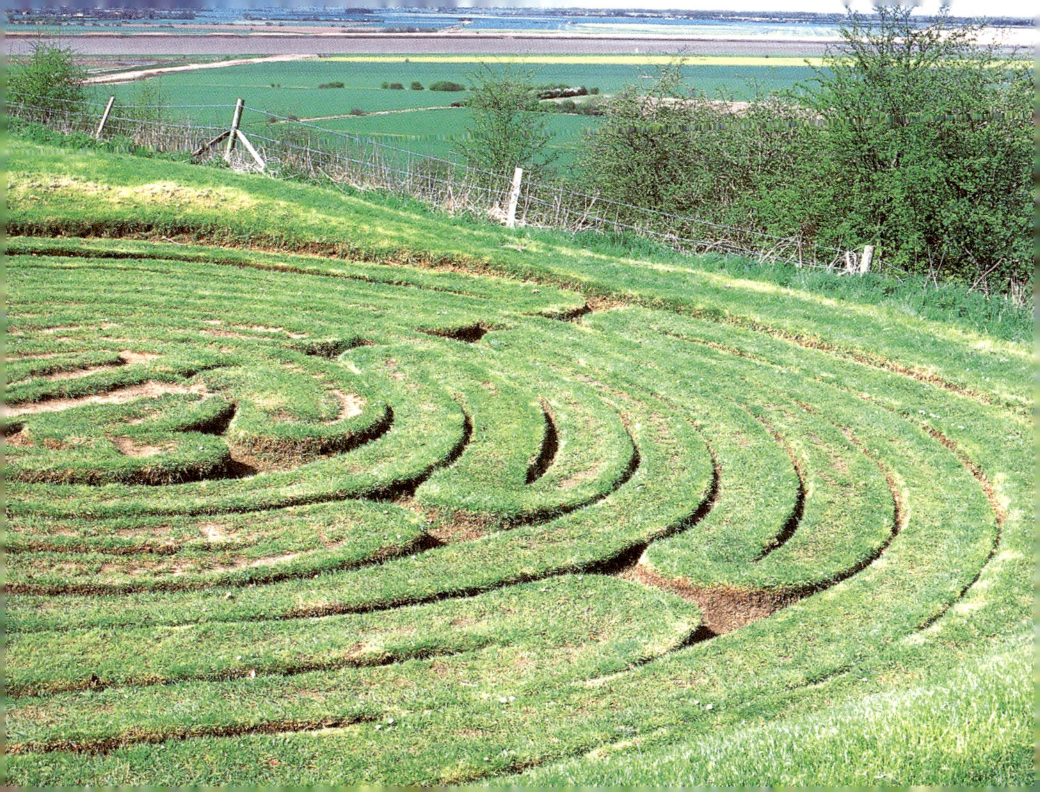

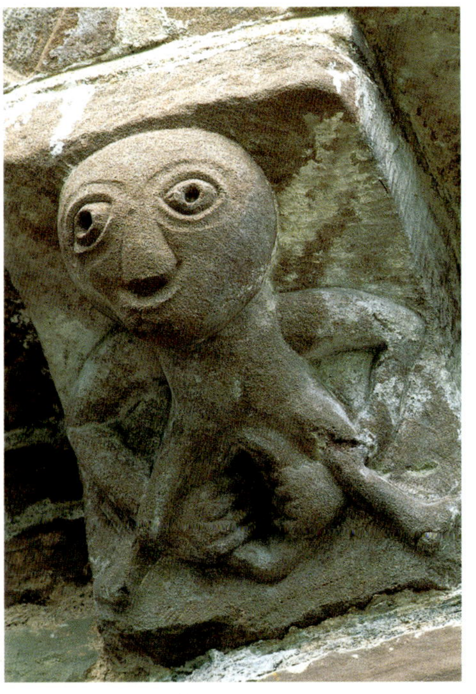

SHEELA-NA-GIG,

Kilpeck Church, Herefordshire

The sacred and profane are often closely associated in holy places. Amongst the riot of carving on this Norman church is a frankly sexual female figure displaying her genitalia. She may be a Celtic goddess or an early fertility symbol, but here she is alongside the symbols of the religion which has supplanted her.

Published in Great Britain by
J. Salmon Ltd., Sevenoaks, Kent TN13 1BB.
Website: www.jsalmon.com. Telephone: 01732 452381.
Email: enquiries@jsalmon.co.uk.

Design by John Curtis. Text and photographs © John Curtis.

Printed in England © 2007

ISBN 1-84640-095-3

Title page photograph: Men-an-Tol, *Cornwall.*
Half title page photograph: Glastonbury Tor, *Somerset.*
Front cover photograph: Stonehenge, *Wiltshire.*
Back cover photograph: Dressed Wells, Tissington, *Derbyshire.*

Salmon Books

ENGLISH IMAGES SERIES

Photography by John Curtis

Titles available in this series

English Abbeys and Priories

English Gardens

English Country Towns

English Cottages

English Landscape Gardens

English Follies

English Villages

English Country Pubs

English Castles

English Cathedrals

English Country Churches

Jane Austen's England

Romantic England

Mysterious England